THE
Crayola
SORTING
BOOK

JODIE SHEPHERD

LERNER PUBLICATIONS ◆ MINNEAPOLIS

Official Licensed Product
Lerner Publications Company
A division of Lerner Publishing Group, Inc.
241 First Avenue North
Minneapolis, MN 55401 USA

For reading levels and more information, look up this title at www.lernerbooks.com.

Main body text set in Billy Infant Regular 24/30.
Typeface provided by SparkyType.

Library of Congress Cataloging-in-Publication Data

Names: Shepherd, Jodie, author.
Title: The Crayola sorting book / by Jodie Shepherd.
Description: Minneapolis : Lerner Publications, 2017. | Series: Crayola concepts | Includes bibliographical references and index. | Audience: Ages 4-9. | Audience: K to Grade 3.
Identifiers: LCCN 2016050980 (print) | LCCN 2016051589 (ebook) (print) | LCCN 2016051589 (ebook) | ISBN 9781512432862 (lb : alk. paper) | ISBN 9781512455724 (pb : alk. paper) | ISBN 9781512449280 (eb pdf)
Subjects: LCSH: Set theory—Juvenile literature. | Group theory—Juvenile literature.
Classification: LCC QA174.5 .S54 2017 (print) | LCC QA174.5 (ebook) | DDC 511.3/22—dc23

LC record available at https://lccn.loc.gov/2016050980

Manufactured in the United States of America
1-41817-23777-3/13/2017

Table of Contents

WHAT IS SORTING?

Sorting is grouping similar objects together.

There are lots of ways to sort! You can sort by color, shape, size, and more.

SORTING BY COLOR

You can sort by color.

What's your favorite color? Try drawing a picture using only shades of that color.

You can sort objects by arranging them from lightest to darkest.

DIFFERENT AND THE SAME

Sorting makes it easier to see how objects are the same and how they're different.

Seashells come in many shapes and textures.

Look carefully at the shell textures. You can draw dots to create texture.

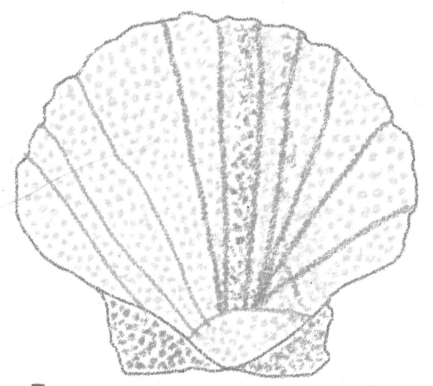

These beads are grouped by shape *and* color!

Draw a picture with big and small shapes in different colors. Can you group them together by shape? Color? Size?

SORT IT OUT!

Sorting cookies and candies is a sweet job! You can sort by type—cake, candy, or cookie. Or sort them by color or size.

You can sort by size from smallest to biggest.
How else could you sort these beach shovels?

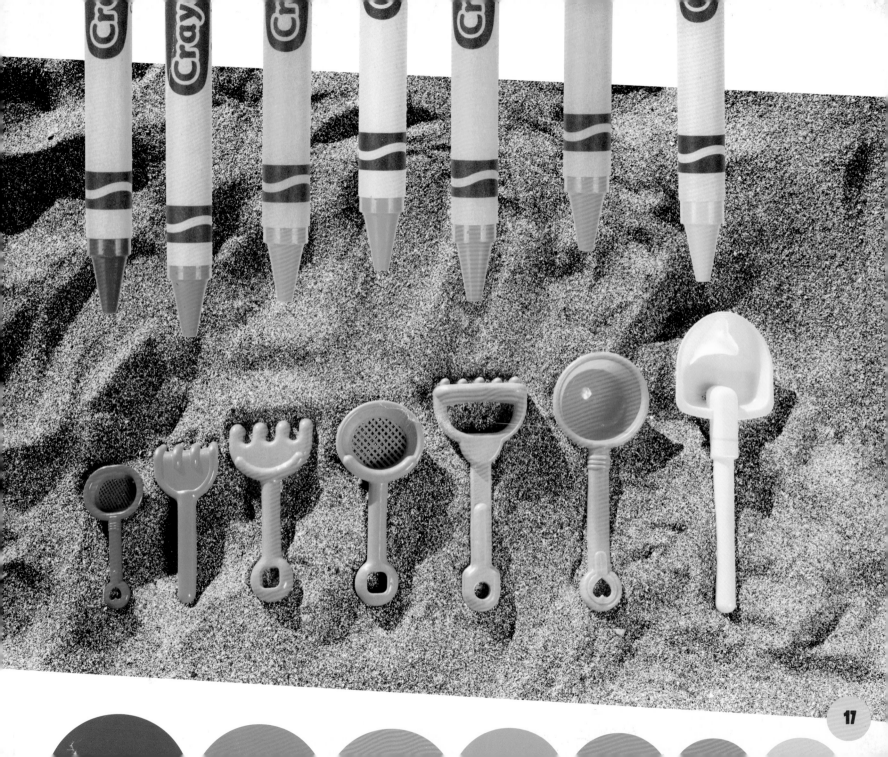

Sorting is a good way to clean a messy room! How do you sort your toys?

Woof! These friendly pups are different in some ways and the same in others. How might you sort them?

WORLD OF COLORS

Here are some of the Crayola® crayon colors used in this book. Can you find them in the photos? Try sorting these colors from darkest to lightest!

SALMON

PIGGY PINK

ROBIN'S EGG BLUE

CERULEAN

SPRING GREEN

SHAMROCK

TAN

SEPIA

GLOSSARY

arranging: putting in a particular order

shade: the level of darkness or lightness of a color

similar: nearly but not exactly alike

sorting: grouping objects together by similarities, such as color or size

texture: the look and feel of an object

TO LEARN MORE

BOOKS

Alexander, Emmett. *Sort It by Color*. New York: Gareth Stevens, 2016. Get extra practice sorting by color with this book.

Driscoll, Laura, and Deborah Melmon. *A Mousy Mess*. New York: Kane, 2014. Read this fun story about a mouse that has to clean up a mess by sorting toys by color, shape, and size.

Flatt, Lizann, and Ashley Barron. *Sorting through Spring*. Toronto: Owlkids Books, 2013. Check out this book to learn more about sorting in nature.

WEBSITES

Counting, Sorting, and Comparing
http://www.abcya.com/counting_sorting
_comparing.htm
Play this fun game to practice sorting by color, amount, size, and more!

Dots, Spots, and Fur
http://www.crayola.com/crafts/dots-spots
--fur-craft/
Draw and cut out animals from real life or from your imagination! Sort them by color, size, or spot type. How else could you sort them?

INDEX

PHOTO ACKNOWLEDGMENTS

The images in this book are used with the permission of: © iStockphoto.com/jallfree, p. 5 (top left); © iStockphoto.com/Nickos, p. 5 (top right); © iStockphoto.com/Spiderplay, p. 5 (bottom left); © Sparkia/Dreamstime.com, p. 5 (bottom right); ©iStockphoto.com/WestLight, p. 5 (center); © iStockphoto.com/Sevulya p. 6; © Andy Piatt/Dreamstime.com, pp. 8-9; © Vesilvio/Dreamstime.com, p. 10; Africa Studio/Shutterstock.com, p. 12; IVASHstudio/Shutterstock.com, p. 15; © Henrik Sorensen/Getty Images, p. 17; © Udra11/Dreamstime.com, p. 19; © iStockphoto.com/Judith Dzierzawa, p. 20; Letterberry/Shutterstock.com, p. 21 (top left); © iStockphoto.com/fstop123, p. 21 (top right); © iStockphoto.com/Panama7, p. 21 (bottom left); liza1979/Shutterstock.com, p. 21 (bottom right); © iStockphoto.com/IgorKirillov, p. 21 (center).

Cover: © iStockphoto.com/GlobalP (dogs); © iStockphoto.com/JacobH (tulips); ©Letterberry/Shutterstock.com (tomatoes).

LERNER e SOURCE

Expand learning beyond the printed book. Download free, complementary educational resources for this book from our website, www.lerneresource.com.